NOTRE DAME

BRIAN LANKER

NOTRE DAME FOOTBALL TODAY

NOTRE DAME FOOTBALL
TODAY

Produced by Rich Clarkso

Foreword by Joe Montana

Essay by Malcolm Moran
The New York Times

PINDAR PRESS ▲ NEW YORK

THE PHOTOGRAPHERS

Brian Lanker

John Loengard

David Alan Harvey

Bob Sacha

George Olson

Kenneth Jarecke

Emmett Jordan

Rich Clarkson

THE STAFF

Publisher: Harvey Rubin

Designer: Bill Marr

Text Editor: Joe Guise

Coordinator: John Heisler

Published by Pindar Press, 12 East 49th Street, New York, New York 10017. All rights reserved. This book, or any portions thereof, may not be reproduced in any form without written permission from the publisher.

First Printing, July 1992

Printed in the United States by Cohber Press, Rochester, NY. Bound in the United States by The Riverside Group, Rochester, NY.

Library of Congress Cataloging-in-publication Data
Notre Dame Football Today/Produced by Rich Clarkson; the photographers Rich Clarkson...(et al.); the writer, Malcolm Moran.
ISBN 0-918223-00-8/Library of Congress no. 92-060931

To order additional copies of *Notre Dame Football Today,* please call 1-800-621-9342, ext. 590.

5

When it comes right down to it, there

probably was no way I was going to end up attending college and playing football anywhere other than Notre Dame. It's the one school I'd thought about attending for a long time. Yet, little did I know at the time just exactly what being the quarterback at Notre Dame would come to mean to me and others around me, even after going on to play at the professional level.

I made official visits to some other schools. In fact, playing college basketball even was a possibility for a time. But I'd grown up with Notre Dame football, and my parents wanted me to go to Notre

RICH CLARKSON

Dame. I knew I couldn't go wrong in terms of the academics. As I recall, there really wasn't much of a decision to make.

I grew up in western Pennsylvania, just south of Pittsburgh in a town called Monongahela. When I was 10 years old, I remember following Terry Hanratty—another western Pennsylvanian—as he led Notre Dame to the national championship in 1966. Another Notre Dame quarterback from the area—Tom Clements—did the same thing in 1973, the year before I enrolled. It seemed I was destined to go to Notre Dame.

The history and tradition of the place was a natural draw, no question. In retrospect, the emotion involved with football at Notre Dame is comparable to anything I've seen in sports. So, if you were Catholic and played quarterback and grew up in a place that embraced the Fighting Irish, who wouldn't want to play football at Notre Dame? I wasn't necessarily one to get outwardly emotional about things like that, but it seemed to be a nice fit.

My career at Notre Dame was not unlike that of anyone else who plays football. There were ups and downs along the way. All I wanted was a chance to prove I could play. There were six other freshman quarterbacks on scholarship when I enrolled, and I just wanted to find a way to get on the field.

There were plenty of high spots for the scrapbooks—comebacks against North Carolina and Air Force in '75 when I first earned a chance to prove myself; the Purdue game in '77 when I became the starter for good; the USC game that year when we first wore green jerseys; the national championship that came from knocking off an unbeaten Texas team in the '78 Cotton Bowl; and then finishing my college career in the cold and ice at the '79 Cotton Bowl with another great comeback in beating Houston.

As a player, you remember the guys you were close to—players like Steve Orsini, Kris Haines, Terry Eurick, Steve Schmitz, Nick DeCicco and Mark Ewald. You never think that much about the magnitude of your accomplishments—individually or as a team—at the time they happen. For a lot of my teammates at the professional level, their memories of victories and great moments from their college years seem to dim as the seasons go by. The amazing thing about Notre Dame is that nearly the opposite seems to be true.

I'm still in awe of the number of people, many with no official ties to the university, who retain such vivid recollections of things that happened at Notre Dame during my playing days. It's been 14 years since I last put on that green uniform. But incidents such as the hypothermia I experienced in the freezing conditions at the '79 Cotton Bowl sometimes seem to take on a life of their own. I'll never forget my bloody elbows and knees that day from the salt on the frozen, artificial turf. There were about 32,000 people who braved the cold at least for a while that day, and I think I've personally met every one of them.

Maybe it's a matter of my continuing involvement with the game of football creating a forum for those memories to reappear. Then again, maybe it's one of those things that's unique to Notre Dame.

There are as many ardent Notre Dame fans in the western Pennsylvania region from which I came as anywhere in the country. Yet, I never cease to be amazed at the constant devotion and unfailing spirit that Notre Dame inspires in its followers.

Maybe that's a part of why I chose Notre Dame. And maybe that's why it's the best move I ever made.

The prestigious Heisman Trophy—emblematic of the top individual in college football each season—has been awarded to Notre Dame players on seven different occasions.

George Gipp doesn't live here anymore. He returns

from time to time, usually somewhere between summer and fall, when the sky is still light deep into the Indiana evening, and the air is still warm, and another football season is about to kick off.

Gipp comes back to see the new, big brick stadium, the one that wasn't built until well after his brief time had come and gone. He visits Washington Hall and strolls down toward St. Mary's Lake to watch the latest generation of young people discovering a place that is old, but new to them.

Gipp looks for buildings of the Notre Dame he remembers and discovers many more he never knew. He is just one solid drop kick west of the brick stadium that somehow, over the years, seems smaller and smaller because of the increased ticket demand. He has found himself in what appears to be almost a village of brand-new buildings, plunked down in the middle of the old. To his left, he can see a gilded dome atop the administration building, but nearly everything else looks so new. He is close enough to Notre Dame Stadium to want to search for echoes, but what George Gipp really needs, at this moment, is an updated campus map.

Just as he begins to feel lost on his own campus, Gipp notices a man in a wide-brimmed hat and a tan three-piece suit.

"Rock? Is that you?" Gipp says.

"George?" the man replies.

How could this be? The wonder of this occasion is that Knute Rockne had not been back to South Bend nearly as often. The coach's brief visits had been reserved for special, desperate moments. He had once inspired a former basketball coach to stretch the bounds of accuracy for the sake of an important halftime talk. He checked out a pep rally the night before a game against Miami, several years

EMMETT JORDAN

back and decided that a modern basketball arena felt too antiseptic for the sweaty business of preparing for a big game. He once helped the stadium flags go limp just as Harry Oliver lined up for a field goal against Michigan. You've got to do what you've got to do.

"You didn't," Gipp says.

"Did you think that was an accident?" Rockne replies.

Gipp knows better. Gipp also understands the image problems he might have faced had he been judged by the scrutiny of the 1990s, the policies directed by the people in the administration building beneath the Dome, and the demands created by celebrity. Gipp has observed the intense attention that Lou Holtz gives to his players on the practice field. He knows he is better off as a part-time visitor and full-time legend because everything appears infinitely more complex than it was in his day.

There is so much for him to tell his coach. There are mobile homes that sometimes appear off the interstates several days before the ball goes into the air. A blimp hovers over the stadium with a television camera inside. Gipp tells of a player named Rocket, with speed that would make the Four Horsemen envious; a receiver, running back and kick returner whose interviews were transmitted to television stations around the world by satellite.

Imagine that. A Rocket transmitted into space.

"He even finished second in the voting for the Heisman Trophy," Gipp says.

"The what?" Rockne says, his eyebrows raised, the lines across his brow growing sharper.

"The Heisman," Gipp says. "Heisman as in Theismann."

"Who?" Rockne says.

This was going to be more complicated than Gipp had thought.

"Rock," he says, "I think we better walk around."

As the two begin their stroll, north and then east, Gipp notices the blue door to the stadium, the one that simply says VARSITY. The sight of the brick stadium and the gold Dome makes Rockne feel as if he had recognized an old friend who never looked so good. Each of the bright gold helmets, repainted before every game, transfers that feeling to a football field.

"A nice touch," Rockne decides. "Now it doesn't matter where the team plays, people will think of that Dome."

The coach also sees buildings where there were once open fields and hears about changes that seem as incongruous to his Notre Dame as nickel backs, cash machines, bowl alliances and pay-per-view telecasts.

For instance, the concept of women at Notre Dame.

"Coeds?" Rockne says. The disdain in his voice made the coach sound as if a kick had just been blocked.

"Coeds," Gipp says. "But they're not called coeds anymore."

The two come upon an area, not far from the administration building, where an open microphone rests on a stand atop a small platform. The microphone provides an informal chance for members of the campus community to address any issue, large or small, to anyone interested in listening.

The issue, at this instant, is personal freedom. A small crowd listens as a woman, in blue jeans and a white peasant blouse, advises incoming freshmen to move into off-campus housing as soon as possible. "Notre Dame means well," she says evenly, "but it doesn't have the right to decide where and how I should live."

Gipp has heard these discussions before. Rockne will need some time to adjust to this public expression. "If I wasn't here," Rockne whispers, "I'd be rolling over in my grave."

Gipp has seen women wait patiently for tickets, as men have done for decades. The women, as they waited, remembered the tiny green footballs they received while still in their cribs. They had returned to school in late summer with specific instructions for their first bookstore visit, including tiny footballs for nieces and nephews, a happy green initiation for another generation. As the women waited in the ticket line, they were convinced that at least once in their four years they would be part of a national

Heisman Trophy winners from an earlier era, Southern California's Mike Garrett and Notre Dame's Paul Hornung meet on the sidelines.

Sunshine, green grass and the return of Fighting Irish fans to campus for a football weekend make for an idyllic September scene on the university grounds.

championship. On Saturday afternoons, their lung power in the northwest corner of the stadium had helped in the effort against Michigan and Penn State and Southern California as much as anyone else's in any other years.

Before the games, the presence of women had added charm to an autumn Saturday. They stand behind grills, next to the guys, as part of a group fund-raising effort to sell food to the pre-game crowds. No matter how big a breakfast you have eaten, no matter how soon the dinner reservation waits on the other side of the final gun, the sales pitch of a freckle-faced freshman—"Pleeeeease" — makes one more bratwurst mandatory on a sunny morning.

What Gipp has learned, along with so many others, is that the first impressions of the place are just that. It's like the Dome — from Exit 77 of the tollroad, day or night, it's a three-dimensional postcard, a familiar sight that marks an arrival at the destination. But you have to come much closer, in the late afternoon, when the reflections from the sunset reveal thin lines in the gold, to begin to understand the texture of the place.

Rockne, or even Frank Leahy, would not recognize the effort that creates the spectacle. The Loftus Sports Center, an indoor practice facility, has computers that design individual exercise programs. An academic support system became a national model from its beginnings in the 1960s. The selection of recruits by the admissions office is part of an obligation that the institution has created for itself.

The obligation, having grown over decades, has become simple even as the world of college athletics has become far more complex. The issue is not a question of whether Notre Dame wins, but how the victories are achieved. That is why small news items can inspire a national discussion, while similar incidents at most other schools might be forgotten by halftime. That is why the graduation rate carries far more significance than public relations value for the recruitment of another class of athletes.

The loyal letter writers, indignant over criticism of their university, should understand one thing about the critics: They also are holding Notre Dame to a higher standard, because if Notre Dame cannot turn an afternoon of collisions on an autumn Saturday into something worthwhile, it is unlikely that any school can.

But if the spectacle is worthwhile, the emotions it inspires can only intensify the sense of being the next link in a very important chain. That is why it is so hard to leave; why Chris Zorich, after his last game in the stadium in 1990, slowly walked the length of the field on a cold, dark night, hand in hand with his girlfriend, long after the game had ended.

The feeling of belonging to something important is what endures even as the physical and emotional landscape has changed, as the buildings go up and the open microphone waits for the next issue to be raised.

This much has not changed: If a high school student becomes enchanted by this place when the sun shines, the flags fly and the band plays over a football weekend, he or she can still be captivated when the snow is knee-deep and spring break is nowhere in sight. No matter when students visit, they often decide the place is well worth four years of their lives.

And when they're here, the place belongs to them, made richer by the return of all those others with degrees or just those subway ties. But almost as soon as the members of the latest generation arrive, it is time to leave and to make a discovery that is as sad as it is inevitable. Sooner or later, Notre Dame belongs to someone else more than it does to them. They thought they had owned the place, but they really were only renting all the time.

Gipp and Rockne are east of the stadium, and Gipp is explaining that it might one day be enlarged or even replaced. The sun has set behind the stadium and the sky is still light, and somewhere off in the distance they hear a rehearsal of the Victory March. Not the whole band, and not even a section. Just a single tuba, preparing for the first game.

Before Rockne leaves, he waits for the tuba to reach the part that triggers the words in his mind: "...wake up the echoes cheering her name..."

Nearly 80 years after he was graduated, Rockne sees that as long as there is room for a freshman class, Notre Dame remains a work in progress.

"I'm going to keep coming back," he says, "until they finish the place."

—Malcolm Moran has covered college sports for The New York Times *for the past 13 years.*

The unmistakable sights and smells of football are ever so prevalent on October weekends as autumn arrives.

Portraits by BRIAN LANKER

RYAN LEAHY
OFFENSIVE LINEMAN, CLASS OF '95

"People hit me with stories

about my grandfather all the time. The amazing

part is that no two are the same. I've heard stories

from professors, ushers at the stadium, people in

church. It seems everyone has a tale to tell,

whether they knew him personally or not. I love it

because I didn't really know him. Each story adds

to the mental picture I have of him.

"Life stopped around our house whenever Notre

Dame was on TV. Then, after the game, my

brother and I would put on these little gold hel-

mets and play football with my dad. I always

dreamed of playing football at Notre Dame."

Notre Dame football includes a unique blend of the old and the new, of history and tradition with the present. Few can appreciate that more than Irish offensive lineman Ryan Leahy, a grandson of legendary Notre Dame Hall of Fame coach Frank Leahy. Ryan's father, Jim, also played football for the Irish in 1968, while his brother, Pat, was a member of the Notre Dame baseball team.

REV. JAMES RIEHLE, C.S.C.
TEAM CHAPLAIN

"I still get sentimental when

I walk around the campus. Most of the freshmen laugh

when I tell them I get tears in my eyes when I hear the

fight song. But, four years later, it's amazing how many

of those students come to me and say the same thing hap-

pens to them. It's difficult not to be narrow-minded or

myopic about this place. I know other places have special

qualities, and I know it's not perfect here, but the spirit is

just unbelievable. There's a sense of family and a sense of

purpose that I've never experienced anywhere else. A lot

of it has to do with the Lady up on the Dome. The reli-

gious element pulls people together on this campus."

Rev. James Riehle, C.S.C.,
believes places such as
Sacred Heart Church
(right) give Notre Dame a
spiritual feeling that is
absent on many college
campuses. A 1949
graduate of Notre Dame,
Father Riehle has served
as chaplain of the athletic
department since 1966.
He also is the executive
director of the National
Monogram Club.

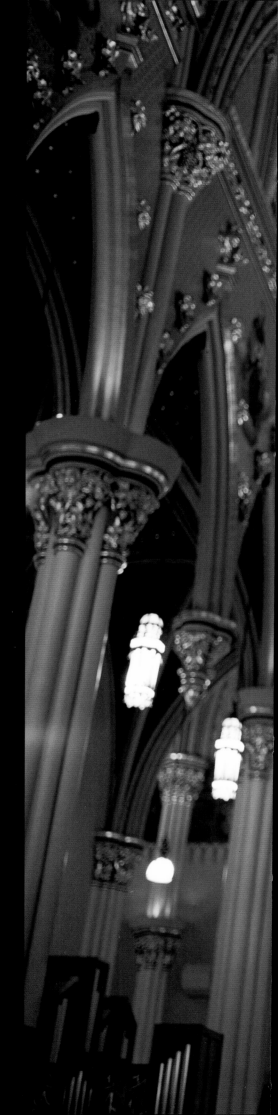

"Notre Dame offers

great opportunities, there's no doubt about that.

We have the most players and the most coaches in

the Hall of Fame, and we have more national

championships and more Heisman Trophy

winners than anyone else. My greatest pride,

though, is in the many academic awards the

program has won. The image of Notre Dame

football was created by Rockne, and I'm proud of

the fact that we continue to respond to the chal-

lenge of upholding that tradition so many years

later."

The old guard of Notre Dame's athletic administration now includes the title "emeritus," but that doesn't mean Col. John J. Stephens (left) or Edward W. "Moose" Krause are any less interested in Irish football fortunes than before. Krause, a freshman in 1930 under Knute Rockne and an all-star lineman, spent 32 years as university athletic director (1948-80). Stephens spent the last 13 of those years as Krause's associate athletic director and sidekick.

DALE GETZ
MANAGER OF ATHLETIC FACILITIES

"Notre Dame football stands for excellence, and

because the team works so hard to achieve its goals, I need to work equally as hard to make sure the facilities are up to their standards. I don't want a coach coming to me and saying, 'Gee, Dale, there was this big divot on the practice field and our top running back stepped in it. He twisted his ankle and now he's out for the season.' That's my worst nightmare."

ROBERT THOMAS
SUPERINTENDENT OF NOTRE DAME STADIUM

"There are times I get so excited for a game day

that I get here at 4:30 in the morning. Every guy on the staff works hard and takes a great deal of pride in his job, whether it's cutting grass or lining the field. The coaches are great about making our crew feel like they're part of the football team. When I go to other stadiums and look at the fields, I honestly feel ours is the best."

The tradition and flavor of 60 years of football at Notre Dame Stadium are shared today by manager of athletic facilities Dale Getz (left) and stadium superintendent Bob Thomas from this, their office and headquarters deep below the stands.

SGT. TIM MCCARTHY

"May I have your attention please...

this is Tim McCarthy for the Indiana State Po

Fans, on the way home, your police officers rem

you to please drive carefully. Ignoring the law

disregarding safety could mean a traffic ticket

a date in court...

MIAMI, 1988

Remember, anytime your driving looks fishy, yo

could be the catch of the day!

MICHIGAN STATE,
1991

Remember, when it's only coffee, there's always

grounds for safety!

INDIANA, 1991

Remember, don't let your day go down the drai

MIKE SEAMON
HEAD STUDENT MANAGER, 1991

"I never slept well on a Friday night. You're *excited about the game, you're thinking about things that could go wrong and how you'll solve any problems that pop up. You want to make sure you have every angle covered. Then from the first moment you wake up until the time you go to bed, all of your energy, all of your thoughts are channeled into Notre Dame football. It's like tunnel vision. When I go to bed on Saturday nights, I'm totally drained. I feel as if I played. I can't imagine what the players feel like after getting beat up and pounded for 60 minutes."*

Among the dozens of invaluable behind-the-scenes workers, the head football manager at Notre Dame has unique responsibilities. In addition to the 55-60 hours a week spent presiding over the details of practice and game weekends, Mike Seamon supervised a staff of 200 undergraduate managers for all 24 varsity sports.

All-star Irish flanker
Raghib Ismail and head
coach Lou Holtz talked
privately on the
University of Miami
practice field during a
Notre Dame workout
prior to the 1991 Orange
Bowl against Colorado.

RICH CLARKSON

SKIP HOLTZ, ASSISTANT COACH

"Mentally, Coach Holtz loves to challenge his players at practice. He'll say something like 'Hey, we all make mistakes, besides I didn't expect you to play much this year anyway.' Now the guy walks away thinking, 'Wait a minute, what does he mean he didn't expect me to play?' That gets under his skin a little and motivates him. You don't have to yell at a guy to get his attention. You just corrected a mistake without yelling, without getting mad, and the player will never make that mistake again."

Some of the best football practice techniques never change. There's nothing better for improving the accuracy of Rick Mirer's passing than a football and a tire.

The end of preseason practice in the August heat means the doffing of shoulder pads and helmets for wind sprints.

Following the season's final practice, the coaching staff and student managers hold their own touch scrimmage—and Coach Holtz ran for a touchdown before the 1991 Orange Bowl.

RICH CLARKSON

LOU HOLTZ, HEAD COACH

"I don't think I smile enough. I get so caught up in games, practices and meetings, and the demands on my time become so great that sometimes I lose sight of the fact that football is fun. I always believed that retirement was the only time to relax and bask in your success. I made a promise at the 1992 Sugar Bowl that I was going to enjoy myself right now. So maybe those pictures of me smiling on the sidelines won't be such collector's items in the future."

Notre Dame's head coach permitted himself a few satisfying moments to enjoy a 1990 victory at Giants Stadium over Navy before moving on to the next week's challenge. He shared the victory with Monte Kiffin, a former Holtz assistant at North Carolina State and Arkansas.

31

For most road games, the football team boards a chartered flight on Friday afternoon. Above, Stuart Tyner leads the way as the fighting Irish head to Giants Stadium for the 1990 Navy game.

JOE O'BRIEN, ASSOCIATE ATHLETIC DIRECTOR

"The plane rides are pretty subdued. Some of the kids are reading, others are studying, some are sleeping. When we land at the airport, that's when things get crazy. It's packed with fans, and there were even times when bands were playing as we came into the terminal. We've had mayors and other dignitaries waiting to greet us. It's quite an eye-opening experience for the players."

Notre Dame executive vice president Rev. E. William Beauchamp, C.S.C., who oversees the Irish athletic scene, visited with members of the football staff as the Notre Dame traveling party winged its way to New York.

Coach Holtz doesn't even relax on the plane. The trip offers valuable preparation time for he and and his wife, Beth.

MIKE SEAMON, HEAD STUDENT MANAGER

"Coach is very quiet on the plane—it's the one time he doesn't have any distractions.

He can really concentrate on his notes for the game, and he can revise his game plan.

He's not worrying about phone calls or visits or dealing with the public."

34

Left: Irish quarterbacks start off the afternoon by watching video of the previous day's practice.

Right: The final 1991 practice before the Sugar Bowl saw Coach Holtz and players alike in a playful mood, part of the relaxed atmosphere that prevailed at the Superdome in New Orleans.

RICH CLARKSON

Room 704 Flanner Hall, 1991-92 home of quarterback Paul Failla, class of '95.

PAUL FAILLA, QUARTERBACK, CLASS OF '95

"I love living with the students and not just athletes because I'm not different from any other student, and that's the way I want it. I enjoy mixing with the rest of the student body. It's refreshing to go back to my room and the hall and not talk football. I can just be a student, and that's what I'm here to be."

RICH CLARKSON

Room 314 Dillon Hall,
1991-92 home of
cornerback Tom Carter,
class of '94.

TOM CARTER, CORNERBACK, CLASS OF '94

"When I come back to my room after a game, people will walk down the hall and tell me I've had a great game. That's a great feeling, knowing the other guys who live in the dorm care. And they're the same way when you get an 'A' on a test. In the dorm, I'm no different than anybody else. My roommate, Derek Flume, and I have lived together since freshman year, and we're best friends. Having a 'regular' roommate, I met a whole new circle of friends, and I built friendships outside football."

Room 516 Grace Hall, 1991-92 home of defensive
end Nick Smith, class of '93, and tight end Irv Smith,
class of '93.

DICK ENBERG, NBC SPORTS COMMENTATOR

"The Notre Dame kids, to a man, are stunning. When you go to a campus during the
fall and talk to athletes while preparing for a game, most of them just want to talk foot-
ball. That wasn't the case with the Notre Dame players. I was amazed at how well
versed they were on a variety of topics and how varied their interests were."

Room 248 Dillon Hall, 1991-92 home of linebackers
Brian Ratigan, class of '93, and Jim Flanigan, class of '94.

KATE HALISCHAK, DIRECTOR OF ACADEMIC SERVICES

"One time I was sitting in the stands and this guy behind me was talking about what an animal Chris Zorich was. Now I know he meant it in a positive way because of how hard Chris played, but it still bugged me. I turned around and told him what a considerate, warm human being Chris was and how seriously he took his studies. Well, this guy looked at me like I was crazy. He didn't want to hear that about one of his defensive linemen. When you see these players off the field, you see them in a different light. They don't just sleep and eat football."

THE LOCKER ROOM

Photography by RICH CLARKSON

Painting the Irish helmets before every game takes time, manpower and fastidiousness from student managers and friends.

When the Fighting Irish arrive in the locker room beneath the stadium on game day, each player's own equipment is carefully arranged in his designated locker. The names at the top of each locker may change from year to year, but the tradition of excellence continues.

CHRIS MATLOCK, EQUIPMENT MANAGER

"I have drawers filled with requests for equipment from fans all over the world. There are two guys from New York who come in once a year and they always ask to take a photo wearing one of the gold helmets. It's incredible how many people just want to touch or see up close something that was used in a game. Everyone wants a piece of Notre Dame football."

During the week, players dress in the locker room at the Joyce Athletic and Convocation Center near the practice fields. **Above:** Quarterback Rick Mirer (3) gets ready for practice.

CHRIS MATLOCK, EQUIPMENT MANAGER

"Some of the players can get pretty superstitious. They like to have their equipment laid out a certain way or they won't give up a particular item. One guy ripped his jersey real bad at practice, but he wouldn't let me give him another jersey. I had to take a shoulder pad lace and tie the shirt together."

The ritualistic dressing and stretching procedures prior to a Notre Dame home game include bits of quiet tension, subdued anticipation and nervous excitement.

Coach Lou Holtz
makes his final speech
to the team before the
opening kickoff.

The Notre Dame
Stadium showers
provide a private spot for
the Irish quarterbacks to
gather before the game.

MIKE SEAMON, HEAD STUDENT MANAGER

"Coach Holtz doesn't pull any surprises during his pre-game speeches. He delivers them all the same way. It's very low-key, calm, business-like, and because he approaches the games that way, it instills an air of confidence in the players. If he ever went into one of those fire and brimstone type speeches, the players would be shocked, and they'd probably have 100 questions. They'd probably be thinking 'Uh-oh, coach doesn't think we're going to win this one!' Coach believes he should not have to worry about these guys getting excited. If they're not pumped up for the game, there's a problem. There are so many things to get them excited: walking down the tunnel, hearing the band, touching the champions sign, those all work better than any rah-rah speech."

LOU HOLTZ,
HEAD COACH

"I spend a great deal of time thinking about what I'm going to say to the players before the game. I usually follow up on a theme I've been developing all week in practice. And while it's planned to a degree, the talk comes from the heart. If you don't speak from the heart, players recognize that."

SKIP HOLTZ, ASSISTANT COACH

"A lot of people probably think the locker room is crazy before a game, you know the image: players screaming, banging the lockers. But it's really very quiet in our locker room. It's like they say in the movie 'White Men Can't Jump,' the players are in the zone. Everybody's getting ready mentally and getting focused. When you talk to players at that point, you can't tell them anything new. You don't want to shake them up. You want to repeat the things you've been stressing all week. If they need to be motivated at that point, you're in trouble. And if they need to learn anything in those last few minutes, you're really in trouble. If a player hasn't grasped what we're trying to do after a week of practice, nothing you can tell him in five minutes is going to make a difference."

The preparation was over but the waiting game continued for the Irish in the locker room as kickoff neared. The three hours of football ahead dominated the pre-game thoughts of Jim Flanigan, above, and Michael Stonebreaker, right.

**JEROME BETTIS,
FULLBACK,
CLASS OF '94**

*"We give thanks to the
Lord before each game.
When you're about to
do battle, it gives you
strength to know He'll
be on your side."*

**RICK MIRER,
QUARTERBACK,
CLASS OF '93**

*"While we're getting
dressed and stretching,
everybody is sort of focus-
ing on what they have to
do individually. The
prayer brings us together
and reminds us that we
can rely on one another
for help. Coach Holtz is
big on family, and when
you're kneeling there
with everyone, you do
feel like a family."*

Left: As the players return to the locker room after pre-game field drills, they receive an individual blessing. Here, Rev. Dan Jenky, C.S.C., presided over the moment.

Right: The great Notre Dame national championship teams of the past are a reminder for players leaving the locker room for the tunnel that leads to the field. Each player gives the traditional clap of the hand against the Champion sign.

Former President
Ronald Reagan made a
pre-game visit to the
Notre Dame locker room
before the 1990 USC
game in Los Angeles.

<u>LOU HOLTZ, HEAD COACH</u>

*"President Reagan dropped by to say hello to the team before the USC game. It was a
total surprise, but he did a nice job talking about how special Notre Dame was to
him when he was a youngster. After that speech, I understood why he was a great
politician. By telling us his feelings about Notre Dame and about his role in the
Gipper movie, he convinced us he was on our side without ever saying who he was
rooting for in the game."*

"Wade Watts, my high school coach, is one of the most influential people in my life. He's the guy who talked me into going to college. All I wanted to do was work in the mill and have a car, a girl and five dollars in my pocket. He taught me to want more out of life. Every time we play at USC he visits the team in the locker room, and this time we presented him with a game ball."

57

FANFARE

A photo essay by John Loengard

ROBERT THOMAS

SUPERINTENDENT OF NOTRE DAME STADIUM

"It gets so loud in the stadium you can't hear yourself think. The noise is at such a level that the goal posts start vibrating."

BETSY CIARIMBOLI, CHEERLEADER,

CLASS OF '92

"It's incredible to start a cheer in our stadium and see the whole crowd pick up on it. Every opposing cheerleading squad that came to games here would always ask us how we got the fans to respond so enthusiastically. They figured we had some sort of detailed practice session with them. But it's just the tradition here. Even the fans work together for the good of the team."

LOU HOLTZ, HEAD COACH

"When MBA students came and asked me if they could do that as a fund-raiser, I laughed because I didn't think they'd get anybody to take a picture. I'm shocked when I hear people crowd around it before games. But I've got to question why they want a photo of me in their homes. That's not exactly a shot you'll see on the cover of GQ."

Football weekends inspire a variety of auxiliary forms of entertainment, including an informal version of ballroom dancing.

LOU HOLTZ, HEAD COACH

"One of these days I'm going to find one of those look-alikes to take my place, so I can run out of the stadium before the game and enjoy all the pageantry and hoopla. I'm so busy preparing and taking care of details that I miss out on the tailgating parties. I've heard it's a pretty wild scene. Just once I'd love to be able to join the fans. They're one of the reasons why this place is so special."

RISH FIRST CHOICE OF GOD

From exotic and luxurious campers to remodeled school buses, Notre Dame fans arrive at South Bend on two wheels, four and more to converge on the parking lots where traditional picnics spice the autumn air with an aroma of tailgate feasts.

LUTHER SNAVELY,
BAND DIRECTOR

*"Our band members are
not music majors and
they don't receive
scholarships. But they
give up a lot of time
because they have a love
for the university and for
the football team. They
take a great deal of pride
in what they do. Their
primary purpose is to
do everything they can
to help Notre Dame
be successful."*

JASON SCARLETT, CLASS OF '92

"They always say the games are great stress relievers, and up until kickoff I'd say that's true. But if you're the type of fan who gets intense at games, like so many of us do, once the game starts you vicariously live that game from the stands. There's nothing relaxing about it. Right before kickoff, the way I feel is you're not just going to a game, you're not just going to win or lose, it's more like we're going to live or die. That's the way I feel. I guess you could say it's a little like going to war."

LUTHER SNAVELY, BAND DIRECTOR

"I'll never forget a game my first year here. Tim Brown scored after a long run. All of a sudden, one of the drummers ran out and hugged him. I really chewed him out for that. Well, he looked at me and said, 'But Tim lives in the room next to me. He's one of my best friends.' You just don't realize how close the students are to the athletes at Notre Dame."

ROBERT THOMAS, SUPERINTENDENT OF NOTRE DAME STADIUM

"One night after a game, I was the last one to leave the stadium. I locked up and went out to my truck to go home. Just before I pulled away, I noticed the lights in the locker room were on. Now I know I turned them off, but I went back in and turned them off again. I get out to my truck the second time, and the lights go back on. I didn't find anybody inside, so I didn't know what was going on. I'm not one to believe in ghosts, but you start thinking about all the stories people tell, and it gets to you. That night I felt a presence in that place. I don't know which legendary player it was, but he certainly didn't want to leave."

Right: Long after the stadium has emptied, South Bend youngsters play their own game of touch football.

The color guard stepping on to the field and the arrival of the Goodyear blimp, a platform for a television camera, signal the start of the Saturday spectacle. The kickoff is near for thousands in the stadium and millions at home.

KENNETH JARECKE

Left: For weekend home games, the parking lot transforms into a village on Friday night and a small city by Saturday morning, and a friendly game of football is liable to break out at any time.

Right: Applying a fresh coat of paint laced with real gold is a longtime Friday night tradition for the spotless Notre Dame helmets.

GEORGE OLSON

MIKE SEAMON, HEAD STUDENT MANAGER

"Painting the helmets each week is a big ritual. Student managers have always painted them, and everyone looks at it as a great privilege. They're one of the most simple helmets in the nation, but they symbolize the Dome and what Notre Dame stands for. After you work so hard on it, it feels great on a sunny day when you see those helmets sparkle and shine. It takes 12 to 15 coats of paint to do it right. The whole process is easily eight hours start to finish. After the helmets dry, they polish them, buff them, shine them up, and make sure the equipment (hinges and facemasks) on them is fine. We put in a lot of work because the helmets are the first thing everyone focuses on when the team comes out of the tunnel.

"Even though everyone has fun, it can get pretty tense at times. Before the Penn State game one year, the paint was freezing before it hit the helmets, so they were turning sheet white. All I could think of was the team running out of the tunnel wearing them that way. It would've looked like an intrasquad scrimmage at Penn State. But we buffed them up with a little turpentine, and that took the white film right off. It's a good thing, too, because I probably wouldn't have lived to see kickoff."

73

BOB SACHA

TONY ROBERTS, PLAY-BY-PLAY ANNOUNCER FOR MUTUAL BROADCASTING

"No other school can match the tradition and spirit of Notre Dame. And you don't just feel it over at the stadium. It's everywhere on campus. People see the Golden Dome and Sacred Heart Church and all the statues. They take a walk down to the Grotto. You know you're in a special place right away. The spiritual feeling there, the sense of togetherness, that's what makes Notre Dame unique."

JESSICA CHIAPPETTA, CHEERLEADER, CLASS OF '92

"Some people say pep rallies are a thing of the past, but that's not the case at Notre Dame. Some fans are just as intense about it as they are about the game. For those who can't get a ticket, it's the big event of the weekend. It gives them a chance to see the players up close, and they always have guest speakers like Rocky Bleier (class of '68) and even Norm from Cheers *(Actor George Wendt, who also attended Notre Dame). And once the band plays the Victory March, it's hard not to get swept up in the emotion. When you go to one of the pep rallies, you see how deeply people care about the team."*

There are different ways to spend a Friday night before games. It's usually standing room only for pep rallies at the Joyce ACC (right), while other fans prefer to say a prayer at the Grotto (above).

RICH CLARKSON

75

RICK MIRER,

QUARTERBACK,

CLASS OF '93

"We go through a relaxation session every Friday night before a game. Coach Holtz turns all the lights off and has us lay flat on our backs. He tells us to relax each part of our bodies. He wants us to feel as though we're sinking into the carpet. I guess it's a little like hypnosis. You'll catch a guy snoring here or there because it's so mellow, but most of the guys take it seriously. When you're a freshman, you think it's kind of weird. But you learn to respect it. It's one way of getting mentally ready for the game. And it's a good way of winding down after a hard week of practice."

Visualizing the next day's game, the players meditate to Coach Holtz's narrative in the dim light of the Loftus Sports Center's exit signs.

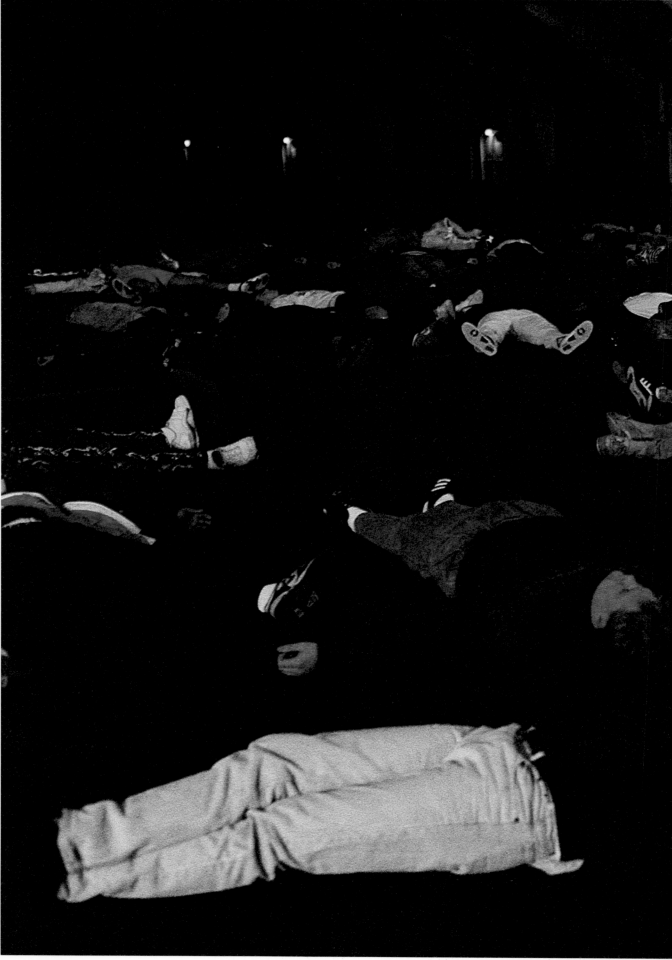

RICH CLARKSON

REV. JAMES RIEHLE, C.S.C., TEAM CHAPLAIN

"We have a team mass before every game. And everybody has to be there, Catholic or not, because it's more of a morale thing. On the road, we used to find a local church, but now we have the mass in our hotel. At the churches, we'd get something like 500 people showing up for mass. It's amazing how many fans want to be there. Sometimes I wondered if opposing fans also showed up to make communion take so long our players would have less time to get ready for the game. Even at the hotel, we have to lock the doors to keep the whole thing from becoming a circus."

RICH CLARKSON

JEROME BETTIS, FULLBACK, CLASS OF '94

"I don't think too many teams are in mass three hours before kickoff, but we all look forward to it because it keeps things in perspective for us. Whether you're Catholic or not, it humbles you to think about someone greater than you, and you need a source of strength to keep working hard day in and day out. It's also great for team unity."

LOU HOLTZ, HEAD COACH

"The highlight of the whole weekend for me is the team mass. Religion has always been the backbone of my life, and I love the spiritual feeling here at Notre Dame. As far as the players go, even if they're not religious, getting together like that is great for morale and character."

In the chapel of Pangborn Hall, Rev. Dan Jenky, C.S.C., celebrated team mass before a home game.

"On Saturdays you see alumni and fans walking by with all their gaudy clothes. Students like to joke about that. But we're not kidding any-body. In a few years we'll be wearing lep-rechauns all over our legs and one of those funny hats—all of the stuff that will embarrass our kids," says Jason Scarlett, class of '92.

NOTRE DAME

FIGHTIN' IRISH

BOB SACHA

BUBBA CUNNINGHAM, BUSINESS MANAGER

"We have one guy who works in our parking concession who lives in Pennsylvania. He comes back for every home game just to park cars. He's done it in the same lot for 26 years, and then he drives home. He doesn't even go into the game."

BOB SACHA

83

BUBBA CUNNINGHAM, BUSINESS MANAGER

"We haven't had a ticket for public sale since 1967, so we always get all sorts of crazy reasons why people should get tickets. One guy sent us some pictures to prove how big of a Notre Dame fan he was. He has a farm in Ohio, and his corn silo is a replica of the Golden Dome. His license plate says, 'Pray the Rosary,' and he has a luggage rack on top with a statue of Mary. He hoped that would make him seem worthy for tickets. I just didn't have any to give him."

DAVID ALAN HARVEY

GEORGE OLSON

JOE DOYLE, SPORTS EDITOR EMERITUS,

SOUTH BEND TRIBUNE

"Jim Murray of the **Los Angeles Times** *once said Notre Dame fans are the string savers of our culture. They hang onto every bit of information or any piece of memorabilia they can get their hands on."*

P. J. GOODWINE,

BAND MEMBER, CLASS OF '92

"I grew up knowing the words to the Fight Song because my brother and sister were in the band. You feel honored to play it because you're carrying on such a great tradition that's been around since the early 1900s. Sometimes you get tired of it, but the reaction from fans is always so great and that makes it exciting. We probably play it around 500 times during the fall."

About two hours before kickoff, the band plays a concert on the steps of the Main Administration Building. "People come to campus and take in moments like that without ever going to the game. I've never been at a school where the band had a following other than parents and friends," says Band Director Luther Snavely.

TOM LEAR, JR., CLASS OF '92

"When you wake up on Saturday mornings, you smell the bratwurst cooking. The campus is packed with people sightseeing, visiting with friends and playing football. The tailgaters are so friendly here. People you don't even know come up to you and say, 'Come on over and have something to eat.' If you've got a Notre Dame sweatshirt on, you're a friend."

Left: Smoke and the aroma of broiling hamburgers and bratwurst flavor the campus on Saturdays before the game as various student groups participate in entrepreneurial money-raising to the delight of alumni and visitors who snack before the games.

Right: Young fans, would-be Joe Montanas, practice the art of Notre Dame football before the Golden Dome itself on game mornings.

RICH CLARKSON

"I live about 75 miles from Notre Dame, but I still come to all the games, and I've been doing that since I was 12. I love the atmosphere here. Everybody makes you feel welcome. For some reason, this place sets you at ease. If you've got some problems, you can come here, enjoy the day and forget about everything for a little while. It's a good feeling."

A statue of Father Edward F. Sorin, C.S.C., founder of the university, stands tall near the entrance to campus.

BOB SACHA

Members of the Irish
Guard exchange stories
as fans await the team's
arrival in the tunnel.

MIKE SEAMON, HEAD STUDENT MANAGER

"Fans hang over the tunnel waiting to see the team. The stadium starts to buzz, you can feel the excitement as you stand there in the tunnel. You're anticipating the roar but for some strange reason you start thinking at that point about all the hard work you put in. You want to cry, you want to yell, you want to burst. You could never be any happier than you are at that moment. It's the biggest rush you can have. Everything you do leads up to that moment when you run out of the tunnel."

Calisthenics mean
that kickoff finally is
within sight.

RICK MIRER, QUARTERBACK, CLASS OF '93

"The only time you really notice what the fans are doing or saying is during the pre-

game warm-ups. They're situated so close to the field at our stadium that sometimes it

feels as if they're standing right next to you."

BOB SACHA

There's little question where this young fan's rooting interests lie.

SEAN GRACE, CLASS OF '92

"The players here are great about giving autographs. They're in the spotlight all the time, and they're under such great pressure, but they still take time to sign for kids and even students in the dorms. It seems as though they are genuinely taken aback by the fact that people care enough about them to ask for an autograph."

Linebacker Demetrius
DuBose obliges a patient
pre-game admirer.

RICH CLARKSON

"Waiting in that tunnel before the game, you always get a big rush of adrenaline. You're excited about going out to do your part, plus you're a fan and you can't wait to see the game. You're also a little bit nervous because you're thinking, 'What if I fall down? The whole stadium will see it.' Sometimes opposing players and even assistant coaches point their fingers and yell at us. In a way, I guess it shows you how much the band and the Irish Guard are part of the football experience here. Why else would the other team take the time to try and intimidate us?"

The Irish Guard stand at attention next to the door of the visitors' locker room just before the game. Here, Southern Cal filed quietly past the Guard.

JEROME BETTIS, FULLBACK, CLASS OF '94

"Running out of the tunnel is the first time that day we let our emotions out. It's an exhilarating feeling, and it takes your breath away no matter how many times you go through there. Your heart starts beating a little quicker, and you get a chill. It's a rush you can't really put into words."

KENNETH JARECKE

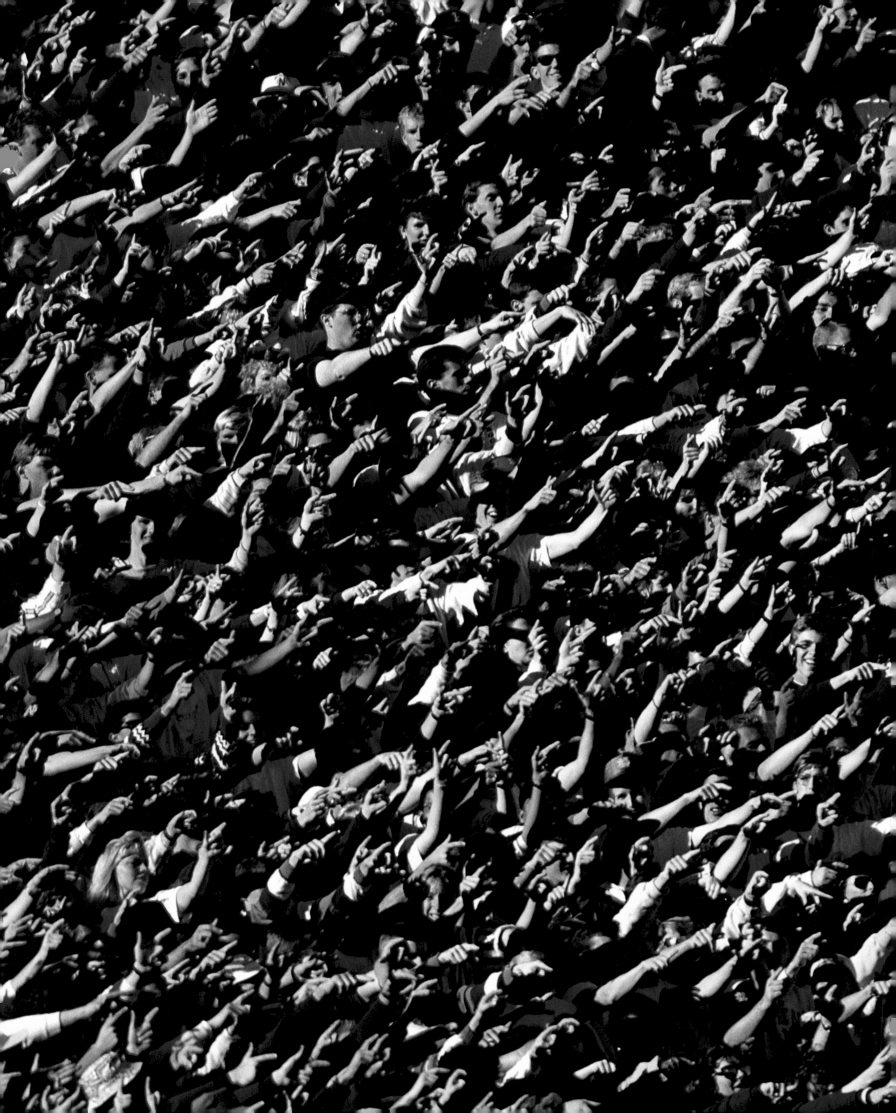

**LUTHER SNAVELY,
BAND DIRECTOR**

*"Before I got here, the
band gave a halftime
show and played the
1812 Overture, complete
with the cannons. The
crowd really loved it, so
the band started playing
a shorter version of it
during the game. At
some point people started
conducting with their
arms. Now we always do
it at the end of the third
quarter. There's no way
you could ever plan
something like that, and
now we'd never think of
not playing it."*

KENNETH JARECKE

103

Not even a broken arm could stop leprechaun Bryan Liptak from entertaining the crowd during the 1990 season.

BOB SACHA

105

ANGELO BERTELLI,

CLASS OF '44

1943 HEISMAN TROPHY WINNER

"I don't think I could even play today. These kids are much bigger and faster than I ever was. They hit the weights religiously, and everyone is so specialized. In my time, the rules said you had to play both ways, but not everyone was great on both sides of the ball. Now you have great people at every position, so the game is much more complex. Watching the way these kids hit, I'm glad my time here came before the modern era."

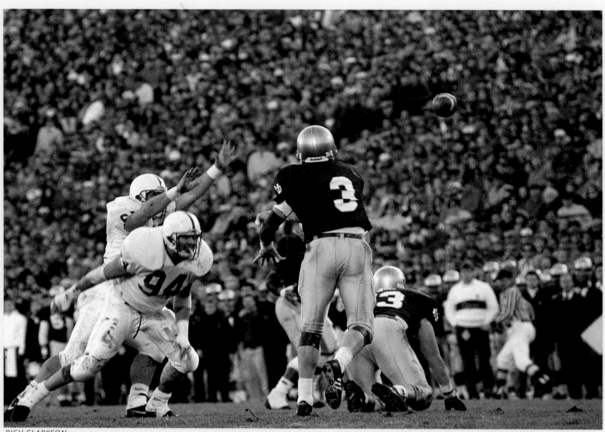

RICH CLARKSON

RICK MIRER, QUARTERBACK, CLASS OF '93

"When you're out on the field during a game, you feel like you're playing in a tunnel. You know the place is packed and everyone is going crazy, but to the players it's like one loud roar, almost like a plane passing overhead. You don't notice anything around you except other players. When you come off the field to the sideline, it's almost as if you step back into reality. That's when you're able to hear and see a little of what's going on in the stands."

Above: Rick Mirer side-steps Penn State's pressure and zeroes in on an Irish receiver.

Right: All eyes were on the football as all-star cornerback Todd Lyght took matters into his own hands.

Mom injects a moment of
frivolity as the band read-
ies for its march from
Washington Hall to Notre
Dame Stadium.

DICK ROSENTHAL, ATHLETIC DIRECTOR, CLASS OF '54

"As a product of the Notre Dame athletic program, as an alumnus and as a fan, I love to see our football team win. But the most important part of my job is to ensure our program maintains its integrity. If we do that, we never have to apologize for winning. We're proud of our athletic heritage, but it's only a part of the university. And we have to remember that football is just one facet of the player's education here."

Right: An Irish victory brought smiles to the faces of (from left) assistant athletic director Brian Boulac, athletic director Dick Rosenthal and executive vice president Rev. E. William Beauchamp, C.S.C.

"It's a challenge for a band director to keep the kids focused on what they have to do here because the games are so exciting and they can get wrapped up in them. But it's a nice problem to have. More than anywhere I've ever been the student body, the band, the cheerleaders and the team all really work together and support one another here."

DAVID ALAN HARVEY

Right: The reaction and facial expressions of Notre Dame's Bob Dahl and Colorado's Darian Hagan give away who got the better of the last play in the 1990 Irish-Buffalo Orange Bowl.

"After big games at home we have had some problems getting Coach Holtz back to the locker room. The fans mob the field, and so many of them want to congratulate Lou personally. Others just want to get on TV," says security guard Paul Harvey.

KENNETH JARECKE

Offensive guard Aaron
Taylor isn't shy about
showing his emotions on
the football field.

GEORGE OLSON

"So many people talk about how excited they get when the team comes out of the tunnel or when the band plays the fight song, but for me there's nothing like the actual game. I get so much enjoyment out of watching our kids on the field because I know how hard they've worked to get to that point. After all the meetings and practices and conditioning sessions, it's nice to see them get the reward on Saturday and have a chance to do something when it really counts. Putting it all on the line during a game, that's what they're here for."

An interception by
Michigan's Vada
Murray in 1990 gave
Irish split end Tony Smith
the rare opportunity to
make a tackle.

RICH CLARKSON

SKIP HOLTZ, ASSISTANT COACH

"If fans walked into the coaches' box during a game, they might think they were in Japan because we don't speak English. It's all football terminology being thrown around. It's not real emotional in there because you're so far removed from the field. You almost feel like you're watching a film."

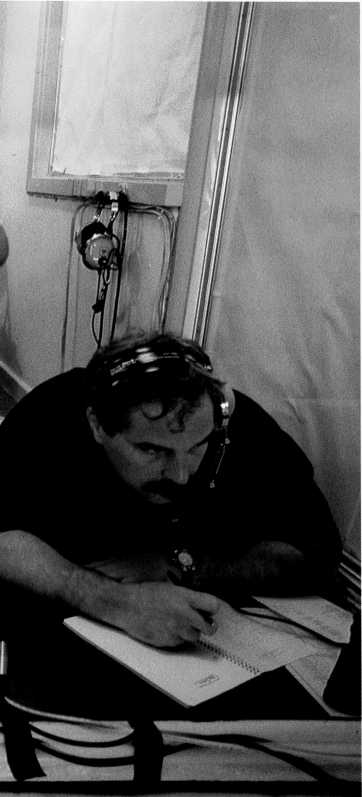

EMMETT JORDAN

EMMETT JORDAN

The Irish coaching brain-trust upstairs relays suggestions to quarterback Rick Mirer (right) during the '90 USC game. "The tough part is trying to hear them through all the crowd noise," Mirer says. "It's not like you're ordering a pizza. You have to really concentrate because the information the coaches give you could determine the outcome of the game."

RICH CLARKSON

BETSY CIARIMBOLI,
CHEERLEADER
CLASS OF '92

"It's so depressing to be on the sideline when the other team is about to win. You pray for a miracle, but deep down you know it's over. It's sad to look over at our players. You can see the disappointment in their faces. They work so hard and they want to win so bad that you know they're devastated inside. You see those faces, and you hurt, too."

Worried Irish players keep their eyes on the scoreboard. From Top: Todd Lyght, Peter Rausch, Raghib Ismail, Derek Brown, Tony Smith and Rick Mirer (right).

SEAN GRACE

CLASS OF '92

"It gets to a point where a running back gets tackled in the backfield and it's like the end of the world. You expect a great play on every snap. You get so wrapped up in the game that you lose touch with reality. You know the team is striving for perfection and somehow you start believing they can achieve it each and every game."

RICH CLARKSON (3)

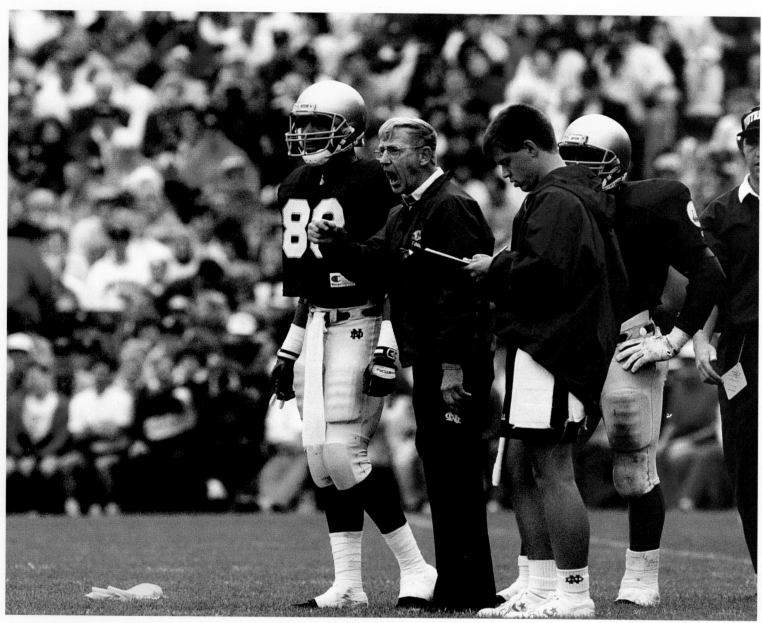

MIKE SEAMON, HEAD STUDENT MANAGER

"During a game, my main responsibility is to stay next to Coach Holtz. When he sends in a play, I write it down on the clipboard. I have the best seat in the house but I miss most of the game. I'm right there when all the decisions are made, but there are times I don't even know the score because I'm totally focused on what Coach Holtz is saying to the players."

126

Above: Defensive tackle Chris Zorich couldn't hide his emotions as he walked off the field following an opponent's touchdown.

Left: A glance at the scoreboard shows why these Irish cheerleaders were so concerned.

SEAN GRACE, CLASS OF '92

"It's not as if people start doing headers off the library when we lose. But when we don't get that last-second miracle to win it, well, it's like a kick in the stomach."

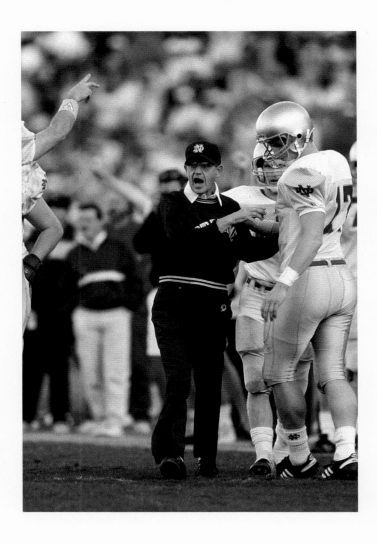

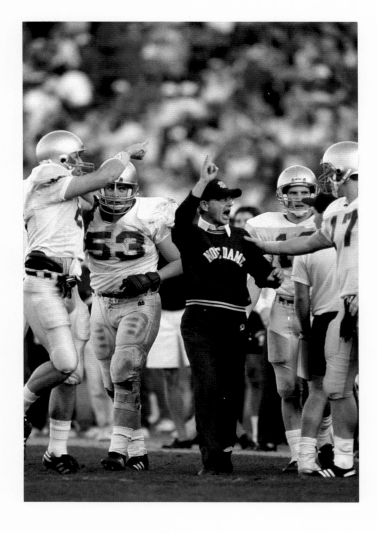

"You can't relax during a game, even if you happen to be winning by a wide margin with a minute or two to go. There are so many things to think about. You want to make sure you get people into the game who deserve it, based on how hard they practice or their eligibility or whose mother and father are in the stands," says Coach Lou Holtz. But in a rare moment of great jubilation, even the head coach jumped into the arms of a surprised assistant following a touchdown drive against Southern Cal.

"As his son, I'm glad to see Coach Holtz showing more emotion. I want him to enjoy his success, step away from it a little bit, get out of the pressure, smell the roses, enjoy being here. Unlike most head coaches, he coaches every position. He wants to be involved in everything. He's going to put himself in the grave, he places so much pressure on himself. But you finally see him throwing the occasional high-five and smiling on the sidelines. He has a long way to go, but he's changing a little, and I'm happy for him."

RICH CLARKSON (ALL)

"Every time you step into that stadium, you're wondering if you're about to see a game people are going to talk about for years to come. You know about the history of the place and all the famous moments of the past, but you want to be part of one as well."

RICH CLARKSON (ALL)

JEROME BETTIS, FULLBACK, CLASS OF '94

"When I score a touchdown in our stadium, I just want to jump up and celebrate with the fans, especially after a long run where I'm overcome with emotion. Once you're in the end zone, at least for a moment, you're able to connect with them. I love sharing moments like that with the fans."

Above: Many Notre Dame fans begin rooting for the Irish at a young age and end up maintaining a lifelong association with the team.

Right: Jerome Bettis' touchdown run against USC in 1991 put the Irish in control for good.

"Coach Holtz was driven by the fact that people were saying we didn't belong in the Sugar Bowl. Take a look at his record. In the games where his team was the underdog, he's almost always won. When you count him out, he's dangerous because he's so driven," says Assistant Coach Skip Holtz.

Below: Lou Holtz reminds George Kelly that, even as the underdog to third-ranked Florida, he felt the Irish could win in New Orleans.

GEORGE KELLY, SPECIAL ASSISTANT TO THE ATHLETIC DIRECTOR, CLASS OF '53

"Going into the 1992 Sugar Bowl, I was very, very skeptical of our chances. So as we walked off the field after the game, Lou was kidding me about that a little bit, and I was admitting he had proven me wrong once again. As much time as I spend with Lou, he never ceases to amaze me. He is one of the great coaches of our time because he has a tremendous aptitude for making young people believe they can do anything. Just when something seems out of reach, he motivates them to grab it. He told me before the game that he felt we were going to beat Florida, even though all the so-called experts said we didn't have a chance. I've learned my lesson. I'll go with his hunches from now on."

133

**KYLE GARLITZ,
CLASS OF '92**

*"It's an incredible feeling to
be down on the field after a
victory. You're high-fiving
and hugging people you
don't even know. You're
jumping up and down, and
then you look up at that
scoreboard. It's amazing. It's
total chaos—state troopers
are running around, the
band is playing the fight
song—but there's no better
way to celebrate."*

KENNETH JARECKE

"When the players come over and raise their helmets to the student body it's like, 'Yeah, we did it together.' It makes you feel as though you had something to do with the outcome of the game. It's a feeling of unity, and you want to reach out and touch the helmets," says Jason Scarlett, class of '92. "Raising the helmets is our tribute to the students," says quarterback Rick Mirer, class of '93. "We want to salute them for being our 12th man. We know how they support us, and it's important for us to recognize their contribution."

KENNETH JARECKE

"Fans want to know everything about the team, so the players today live under a microscope. The coverage now is so much more detailed. It's not enough to describe the game anymore. Now everybody wants to know what a player or Lou Holtz was thinking at every key moment."

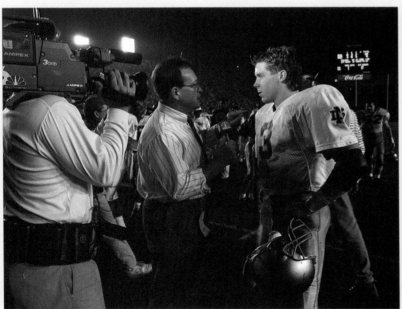

RICH CLARKSON

Quarterback Rick Mirer responded to the questions of Jeff Jeffers of WNDU-TV in South Bend. "It takes a little time to get used to the media attention you receive here," Mirer says. "There's no way any kid who comes in here can be prepared for it. It can get frustrating because reporters come at you in waves. Each person wants to get a different quote, so you end up answering the same question dozens of times." In addition to local and national television, Notre Dame is seen on live television across Europe and in Japan, complete with translated play-by-play.

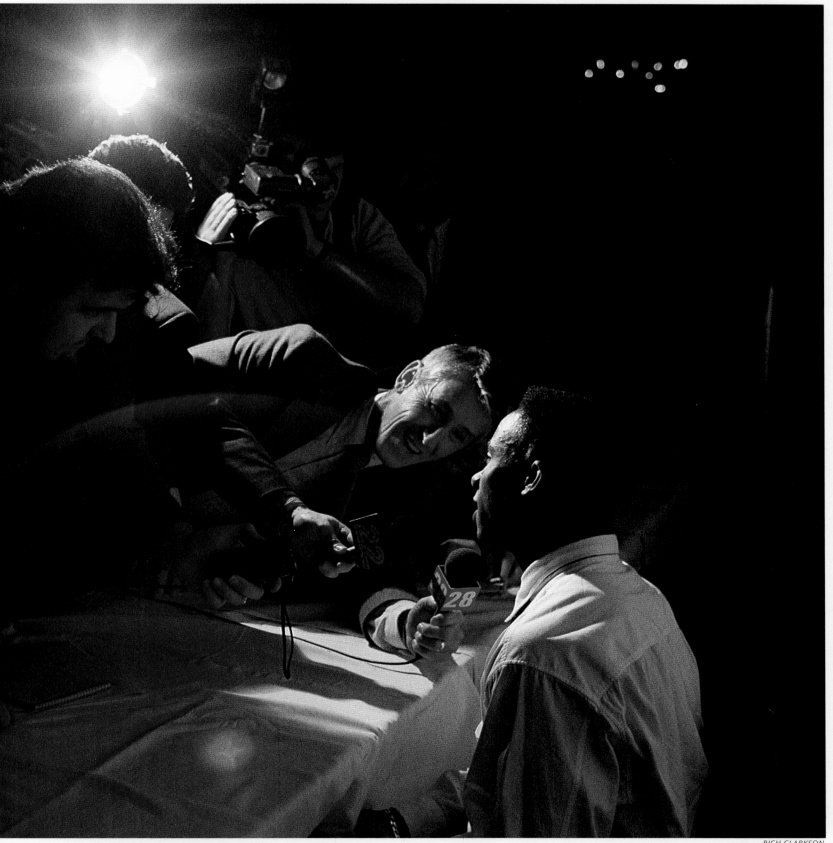

RICH CLARKSON

Notre Dame Heisman candidates always seem to attract the most attention, as did Raghib Ismail. He was runner-up in the 1990 balloting, but reporters still gathered around him at the Downtown Athletic Club in New York City.

KYLE GARLITZ,
CLASS OF '92

"From September to Christmas break, football games are the biggest social events on campus. It's the one thing that brings all students together. You have to hit the books all week, so football helps you get by. You can blow off steam. It helps everybody relax."

BOB SACHA

142

Over the past 25 years, Notre Dame football has drawn me to South Bend many times to photograph Fighting Irish games. As a *Sports Illustrated* contributing photographer, I have been to seven bowl games in which the Irish have played and have witnessed three national championships.

At the same time, I have visited other college campuses across the nation and seen countless other games, but I have always looked forward to Saturdays in South Bend. Notre Dame football represents a proper quest for great achievement while keeping the game in perspective.

In 1989 I organized a photographic book about college football across the nation, "Game Day USA," which looked at the teams, the faces, the bands and all that makes college football unique in the American experience. Of course, we visited Notre Dame for that book.

But it was the next autumn, when the book was published, that John Heisler, Notre Dame's sports information director, called to ask if I would consider doing such a book about Notre Dame. I didn't have to be asked twice.

For two years, I photographed the ins and outs of Notre Dame football. To add more perspective, we asked six other major photographers to travel to South Bend to bring their insight, talent and variety to the project. And after visiting with Malcolm Moran into the wee hours at "Gipper's Lounge" at the end of a Notre Dame weekend, I realized that *The New York Times* collegiate football writer has a unique understanding of Notre Dame football.

This project never was anything less than pure fun. And it was made even more enjoyable by the quality of people in the Notre Dame athletic and academic family, many of whom assisted with the production of this book. Certainly John Heisler and his assistants, Jim Daves and Rose Pietrzak, were always helpful, often in the midst of a media swirl that always encircles Notre Dame. Coach Lou Holtz accorded a behind-the-scenes access he has never before granted. Others on the staff were always willing to lend a hand, including George Kelly, who seems to organize almost everything; senior student managers Shawn Wilks and Mike Seamon, who are given responsibilities unique in college football; athletic department chaplain Rev. Jim Riehle and the late Gene O'Neill, who was Notre Dame's longtime equipment manager. In fact, everyone at the school was extremely cooperative when it came to this project.

Designer Bill Marr joined the effort for the third book on which we have worked together, providing both beautiful design and insightful editing advice. Emmett Jordan, my associate, provided countless moments of help along with some fine pictures.

And finally, publisher Harvey Rubin and his editor, Joe Guise, not only joined the project with enthusiasm but committed extra efforts to produce a book on the finest paper available with superior printing and binding—a special commitment to excellence.

It fit Notre Dame perfectly.

–Rich Clarkson

BOB SACHA

THE PHOTOGRAPHERS

Rich Clarkson
former director of photography for the National Geographic Society and longtime contributing photographer for *Sports Illustrated;* director of photography for the widely acclaimed *A Day in the Life of America;* producer of the celebrated book *Game Day USA*.

David Alan Harvey
former Magazine Photographer of the Year and one of *National Geographic's* top photographers for more than 20 years; exhibitions of his work have appeared throughout the country.

Kenneth Jarecke
won top photographic awards for his coverage of the Persian Gulf war; also covered the student demonstrations in China, the 1988 U.S. presidential campaign and the Iran-Contra hearings; his work appears in *Life* and *Time* as well as many international magazines.

Brian Lanker
Pulitzer Prize-winning photographer whose book *I Dream a World* presented portraits of America's most respected black women and is one of the top-selling photographic books of all time; one of five photographers to win the National Newspaper Photographer of the Year award twice.

John Loengard
won fame for his classic essays in *Life*, but is equally renowned for his books of criticism and commentary on famous photography; *People* magazine's first picture editor, he held the same position at *Life* for nine years, spearheading the magazine's rebirth as a monthly.

George Olson
an accomplished freelancer whose work appears in *Sports Illustrated, National Geographic* and *Smithsonian;* served as director of photography for the book *Baseball in America*.

Bob Sacha
a premier New York illustrative and editorial photographer who is a regular contributor to *Time, The New York Times Magazine* and *Sports Illustrated*.

Emmett Jordan
joined this project assisting with the editing, production and photography. Previously, he was director of photography of the *Sarasota* (FL) *Herald-Tribune* and a staff photographer on the *Boulder* (CO) *Daily Camera*, the *L. A. Daily News* and the *Arizona Daily Star*.